DISCARDED
from
New Hanover County Public Library

ISRAEL: THE FIRST FORTY YEARS

THE FIRST

Charles Scribner's Sons · New York

ISRAEL
FORTY YEARS

Edited by William Frankel

Copyright © 1987 by Thames and Hudson Ltd, London
Introduction copyright © 1987 by Abba Eban
First published in the United States by Charles Scribner's Sons

All rights reserved. No part of this book may be reproduced or
transmitted in any form or by any means, electronic or mechanical,
including photocopying, recording, or by any information storage
and retrieval system, without permission in writing from the Publisher.

Charles Scribner's Sons
Macmillan Publishing Company
866 Third Avenue, New York, NY 10022
Collier Macmillan Canada, Inc.

ISBN 0-684-18904-6

Macmillan books are available at special discounts for bulk purchases
for sales promotions, premiums, fund-raising, or educational use.
For details, contact:

   Special Sales Director
   Macmillan Publishing Company
   866 Third Avenue
   New York, NY 10022

10 9 8 7 6 5 4 3 2 1

Designed by Ruth Rosenberg
Photo research by Patricia Strathern, Magnum Paris
Printed and bound in Italy by Amilcare Pizzi, S.P.A.

DISCARDED
from
New Hanover County Public Library

NEW HANOVER COUNTY PUBLIC LIBRARY

CONTENTS

INTRODUCTION by Abba Eban

THERE is a paradox and contradiction in every part of the Israeli experience. Israel is both very old and very young. Its continuous memory carries it back to the dawn of recorded history when a small people of shepherds and farmers emerged into independent existence in a small notch of stony territory between the Nile and Euphrates. The Hebrew tribes, according to the biblical story and all other evidence, came out of Mesopotamia and by the time of their conquest of Canaan had long been steeped in the culture of Egypt where their leader Moses was born. But the home in which they settled and which they were to endow with eternal fame was never firmly integrated into either of the two river empires. After their birth in Babylon and their sojourn in Egypt, we find the Hebrews struggling for a fragile but memorable lease of national freedom in a corner of the land between the Nile and the Euphrates, serving sometimes as bridge, sometimes as wedge between the two; living in the shadow of one or the other – but ultimately surviving and outshining both.

A pervading sense of this antiquity strikes the visitor's eyes and heart all over the modern land. It is written prosaically on the signposts announcing the junction between cities: Jerusalem to Jericho and Hebron. Many pious tourists are moved to astonishment by the thought that such places really exist in the mundane world of traffic control. The sense of the past finds a more meaningful and evocative expression in the buildings of the Dead Sea Scrolls which accommodate writings two thousand years old, containing the oldest inscriptions of biblical texts discovered in caves in the Judean wilderness nearly four decades ago. Here and there we find excavation sites where young Israelis volunteer for assisting archaeological digs; they illustrate the passion of a dispersed and uprooted people to discover its ancestral sources. Above all, the Hebrew language, wonderfully enlarged and adapted to every modern use, creates a link between the new Israel and its ancient glory. In many respects, the revival of the Hebrew language is the most astonishing of all the Zionist accomplishments. It is certainly without parallel. It confirms that Israel is not a new esperanto society writing its history on a new slate. It is the lineal descendant of the kingdoms in which Isaiah preached and the psalmists sang their songs of exaltation and despair. It gives Israel's culture a dimension of association and memory which hardly any of the new Third World countries can emulate or contrive. It also has significance in the context of the weary and inexhaustible political polemic. Israel's adversaries often accuse Israel of 'intrusion' into Middle Eastern life. They speak of its alleged 'artificiality' and 'alienation' from the authentic mainstream of the region's life. The truth is that of the 165 states in the international community Israel is the only one that reveres the same faith, speaks the same tongue and inhabits the same land as it did three thousand years ago.

There is, of course, some danger in this rapturous devotion to the ancient past. It sometimes produces a messianic fundamentalism, as if modern Israel is committed to the precise reconstruction of Solomon's kingdom in regional and international conditions which are vastly at variance with those of the past age. It sometimes acts as a barrier to the need for innovation and change. It could be – and actually is – sometimes invoked as an instruction from history to renew the Temple sacrifices which would look crude and incongruous to any modern aesthetic perception. It has already 'inspired' some young Israeli religious zealots to attempt the destruction of the Muslim mosque in Jerusalem (the Dome of the Rock) on the grounds that the Jewish temple must be re-established in its original site, which happens to overlap with the place where the Muslim holy places now stand. Moreover, the intense concentration of Israeli minds on biblical history encourages many citizens to escape from the uncomfortable consciousness that a large part of the history of the land has been written with a strong accent on immutable facts that have been created in post-biblical times. These facts also are part of Middle Eastern history, but are not always recognized as such by all Israelis. A historic consciousness untempered by rationality can easily lead to exclusiveness of pride and consequent irredentist claims. Yet the majority of Israelis are capable of inheriting their history without worshipping it, and the traces of forefathers whose voice and actions once reverberated in these landscapes has an ennobling and refining effect on the national culture.

A T the other end of the time-scale Israel represents the theme of modernity. Its scientific and technological manpower is a distinctive asset in a region where most of the advanced scientific skills still have to be imported. It is usual for governments to support science and technology – which they rarely do in adequate measure – for the sake of the material aid that they bring to the national security and economy. But quite beyond the concrete benefits that Israel inherits from its devotion to the modern scientific enterprise, there is a direct influence on the nation's intellectual shape. Zionism, the national liberation movement of the Jewish people, is not an exclusively Jewish movement. It has roots in the Jewish piety which made the ancient land a focus of anguished longing during the long night of the dispersion. No matter where they lived, Jews were consumed by a sharp nostalgia for the land in which they had known their only brief era of self-expression. 'May my eyes behold Thy return in mercy to Zion.' 'Gather in our dispersed ones from among the nations and assemble our exiles from the corners of the earth.' For century after century the pathos of these and countless other incantations resounded from homes and places of worship in every continent where Jews were scattered. But the prayer for redemption was often accompanied by a steadfast resolve to do nothing to bring about its fulfilment. Indeed, the reliance on divine action to bring the Jews back to their homeland served for centuries as a substitute for action. If God or the Messiah or Providence is going to secure the Return, there is logic in passivity and quietism. So the Jews were not averse to remaining in their places of exile, whether these were in the teeming villages of the Russian Empire where they dwelt in ghettos totally alienated from the neighbouring gentile societies; or in western Europe where they became charged with urgent and creative vitality after the American and French Revolutions and the Napoleonic wars; or in the lands of Islam where the casbahs and mosques were a cold but familiar environment. When poverty and intolerance made their lives unbearable, they were more disposed to seek their salvation in America than in the Ottoman Turkish empire, of which their Land of Israel was an obscure province. What made Zionism a viable option even for the few was the accretion to Zionism of ideas and values that came from outside the Jewish context. Liberal nationalism inspired Zionism's founder, Theodor Herzl, to project the vision and blueprint of a 'Jewish State' which he envisaged as something like a modern secular European republic. Scientific rationalism, born of the Enlightenment, captured the Jewish world, which became free from the hold of mysticism and belief in miraculous redemptions. Chaim Weizmann, who symbolized the scientific dynamism of the twentieth century, led Zionism to its decisive turning-point when in the years 1917-1920 he persuaded first Britain and then the League of Nations to write the idea of the Jewish 'national home' into the politics and law of the post-war international community. This has been described by diplomatic historians as the last victory of persuasion without power in modern international history. David Ben-Gurion was the messenger of pioneering socialism when he took the leadership of the Zionist enterprise after the Second World War. Thus, Jewish nationalism is a composite and original idea, reflecting the particularity of a nation that seeks both to live within its own Jewish legacy, land, tongue and tribal memories – and also to take part in the wonder and innovation of the wider world.

While the Jewish masses were seeking American shores, a sufficient number of Zionist pioneers to create the nucleus of a new society had reached Palestine by the middle of the twentieth century. It was a unique and fascinating spectacle. The 650,000 Jews who lived in the 'national home' at the end of the Second World War had neither wasted their opportunities, nor made the most of them. They were not yet powerful enough to impose their will on their surroundings, but they were too strong and coherent to be ignored or handed over to the vengeful disposition of the Arab world. What made this betrayal impossible even for the permissive conscience of the world community was the fact that Jewish history had become dominated by its most immense and tragic event. The extermination of six million Jews in Nazi-controlled Europe had taught the Jews something about the necessity of power and the vulnerability of homeless exile as a way of life. The Jews now enacted their symphonic transition – from weakness and despair to sudden consolation; from the holocaust to the rise of the Israeli state within a few years of each other.

THE generation which witnessed these two events at first hand is passing on. Their heirs and successors in Israel live on a lower slope of emotional intensity. They read about the Holocaust in the books – sometimes the same books as those which recount the story of the Inquisition and the Russian pogroms. Sometimes they are jerked into a more intimate and terrible encounter with the Holocaust by a particular event, such as the Eichmann Trial of 1962. Similarly, the new generation comes into a world in which Israel's sovereign flag has always existed. Israel was the 59th member of the United Nations; there are now 165. The tragedy and triumph of the late 1940s are a part of memory for young Israelis, not of experience. The national mood is more down to earth, less rhapsodic and much less fearful. The great infusion of manpower in the early years of statehood when the Jewish population doubled itself by immigration in two and a half years is enviously recalled. There is not enough immigration to Israel these days, and far too much emigration. 'Sabras', the native born, are now the overwhelming majority of Israel's citizenry. But there is still no dull uniformity. Just as Israel's geography is marked by a stunning diversity, with hills and valleys, verdant splashes and yellow wastes, a turbulent Mediterranean Tel-Aviv and an austerely reserved Jerusalem with two different climates and temperatures within a few dozen miles of each other – so does the Israeli population still carry the mark of its diverse origins. The word 'gap' still recurs obsessively in Israel's self-description: the gap between European immigrants and the sephardim from Muslim lands; between the generation of the founding fathers and the more pragmatic unexcited youth; between the religious zealots tightly bound by tradition and the secular majority with its quest for easy-going mutual tolerance; between organized labour and the increasingly powerful commercial and industrial sector; between those who look upon the surrounding Arabs with the eyes of Joshua the conqueror, and those who would prefer to live in the terms of the gentler lawmakers and prophets who preached universalism and equality. The diversity is so sharp that some fears have often been expressed about the sheer prospect of solidarity and survival for such a varied tapestry. Yet when all the barriers, gaps and divisions which separate Israelis from each other are laboriously narrated, the overriding impression is one of coherence and solidarity. The scientist from America, the banker from Germany, the labourer from Yemen, the Zionist pioneer from a youth movement in Britain, the violinist from the Soviet Union, the doctor from South Africa, the kibbutznik from Uruguay, the close-knit family from Morocco have all been touched in diverse ways by the Jewish destiny and experience. The reality is that they are here and nowhere else. Israelis may tear themselves apart in virulent political debate and in every expression of competitive grudge, but when the challenge comes through danger from outside threat, Israelis join their hands and hearts in common action and in the unifying memories of recent martyrdom, without necessarily sharing common thoughts or memories.

THE existence of a problem does not necessarily imply the existence of a solution. This elusive fact has pursued Israelis in the most crucial and sensitive area of their concern. For some decades, there was a fatalistic temptation to regard Arab hostility as uniform, incurable, implacable and beyond hope of reconciliation. This sentiment explained both the hard, defiant temper of Israeli life and the ingenuity whereby a society learns to sublimate its weaknesses into reactive strength. In a sense, Arab hostility has been the architect of modern Israeli power. Nothing but stark physical danger would have induced Israel, long nourished in the pacific and pastoral ideologies of European Zionism, to develop the most formidable military force ever assembled by a small nation. The exclusion of Israel from neighbouring Arab markets forced it to seek and find sources of supply and facilities of purchase all over the open world. The result is a commercial network and an industrial-technological infrastructure far more akin to Switzerland and Japan than to a typical Third World economy. The solidarities which have held Israeli society together against its own disruptive tendencies also owe a great deal to necessities imposed by peril, as well as to impulses of positive mutual affection. Israel has paradoxically been saved from hard political choices by the unswerving resistance of Arab leadership to compromise and negotiation. The characteristic Zionist and Israeli response to a proposal of which thirty percent is favourable is to put the thirty percent into the Israeli pocket and to argue about the rest. The typical Arab and, particularly, the Palestinian reaction to plans and proposals which are eighty percent favourable to them has been to throw the entire proposal into the fire. Arab leadership has rarely lost a chance of missing an opportunity. Those who ask for all or nothing are more likely to get nothing than to obtain all. Arab initiatives or attitudes led to wars which always ended in tangible Arab loss and to Israeli gains which, in general, Israel had been willing to live without, had that option existed.

This pattern changed sharply after the wars of 1967 and 1973 in which Egypt had led the Arab world. In 1967, Egypt had seemed to be on the verge of carrying out the dream of eliminating the Jewish presence from the Middle Eastern map. In six extraordinary days Israel had repelled the danger, broken out of siege and added all of the West Bank, Gaza, Golan and Sinai to its control and jurisdiction. In the Yom Kippur war of 1973 Egypt under Anwar Sadat had made an impressive but unsuccessful attempt to restore Arab losses and to strike a mortal blow against Israeli forces. In the ensuing years Sadat made a daring appraisal of past Arab errors, bravely jettisoned the literature and rhetoric of Arab anti-Zionism, and reached a peace treaty with Israel with American mediation. Egypt regained the whole of Sinai, including airfields, oil deposits, a naval base and Israeli settlements which had been hopefully established on the assumption of long-term Israeli control. Israel, for its part, achieved a historic breakthrough towards a peaceful relationship with the Arab world. A new window was open and the fresh air came rushing in. With Egyptian oil flowing into Israeli tanks and tankers, with buses from Israel setting out for Egypt each day, with Israeli and Egyptian aircraft landing in each other's airports, a new vision of regional order presented itself to Israeli and Arab eyes.

It was hoped, and sometimes even believed, that this far-reaching event would inaugurate a parallel process of reconciliation in other sectors of the conflict. Largely owing to Palestinian intransigence this prospect was not fulfilled. But the vision has not been completely lost, and embattled defiance may not be Israel's only destiny.

I T is here that the story ends for the time being in an atmosphere of ambiguity. The Six Day War of 1967 is the formative date in Israeli history. Most Israelis divide their experience between what happened before that date and what ensued thereafter. Now, on the twentieth anniversary of the Israeli victory and the resultant Israeli rule over 1,300,000 Palestinian Arabs and their densely populated areas of habitation, it appears that there may have been a crucial failure to understand the limitations as well as the potentialities of that victory. It was a spectacular military triumph which has had a durably tonic effect on the nation's confidence. It was also a political gain, investing Israel for the first time with a real negotiating capacity. Egypt would not have made peace with Israel if Israel had not possessed assets which it could either retain or confer. But the Six Day War was not a messianic dispensation. It did not put the future in Israeli hands. The Arabs continued to deploy their basic resources, and the geopolitical power balance in the Middle East was not profoundly changed. The Arabs still exceeded Israel in territory, population, multiplicity of sovereignties, oil, money and strategic importance. Above all, they retained the power of refusal. Israel could not dictate the settlement; it would have to negotiate it.

The trouble was that Israeli exuberance had soared to a height at which this realism sometimes disappeared from view. One Israeli general, later to become a senior minister, had declared that 'Israel could now capture the entire area between Pakistan and Libya'. This was a few weeks before the Yom Kippur War when Israel was fighting hard for Tel-Aviv and Jerusalem! Other Israeli slogans were: 'We have better boundaries than David and Solomon'; 'Time is on our side'; 'There is no such thing as the Palestinian people'; 'We shall build a deep water port in Sinai'; 'The Arabs have no military option.' Meanwhile fundamentalist movements proclaimed universal Israeli possession over every inch of soil in the Land of Israel and told the Arabs that they could either submit to permanent Israeli rule without political rights for themselves – or remove themselves to other lands. Not all Israelis were infected with this arrogance, but the effects of militant ideologies and the actuality of ruling a foreign subject nation have certainly diminished the lucidity, vision, compassion and honest self-appraisal which marked the thought and conduct of those who brought Israel out of the wilderness into the promised land.

The population of Gaza alone is now 600,000 Arabs. In Israel plus the West Bank and Gaza there are more Arab births than Jewish births each year. If this situation is perpetuated through deadlock or diplomatic inertia, Israel will soon have to ask itself a searching question to which there are no answers without pain. Shall Israel accord equal rights and franchise to the Arab population in the West Bank and Gaza? In that case, Israel will lose its majority status and will become yet another Arab state without Jewish control of its legislation or policies. Or shall Israel hold on to the 1,300,000 Arabs without granting equality of status and the right of participation in the central political system? In that case, Israel will lose its status as a democratic nation and will become a society in which a man's rights are defined by his ethnic origin. This would lead to the grand anti-climax: the people that first enacted the law of social equality, 'One law shall there be for you and for the stranger', would become its most prominent violator. As Israel approaches its fifth decade the shift of priority has thus passed from the issue of physical defence to the issue of structural coherence. In Sinai and Lebanon Israel has enhanced its security by disengagement and deterrence without pushing its power into the very face of its adversaries. In the Israeli-Palestinian dialogue the problem is more complex. It will not be easy for Israelis to abandon their control over areas rich in ancient historical meaning and to trust their future to demilitarization, peace and territorial restraint. But it is reasonable to assume that most Israelis would take that risk, trusting in their immense military preponderance, if only Arab moderation made this a concrete option. Israel is a sovereign state; but it is part of the paradox of the times, as it is throughout the international system, that a nation's destiny is determined not by its unilateral will as much as by its capacity to seek harmony between divergent interests and values.

WHEN all is said and written Israel's rebirth is a great and noble adventure. Never before have a people, a land and a language long separated and dispersed come together again in a great sweep of historical continuity. The hard dilemmas that Israel will have to resolve within the few coming years will, at least, be confronted from a condition of greater strength and confidence than the Jewish people has ever commanded throughout its history. It faces an Israeli population, an international community, a Soviet Jewry awaiting salvation and an Arab world in the torment of new ideas in the knowledge that there can be few perils in Israel's future greater than those overcome in the past. Its mandate remains constant: to serve the interests of the Jewish people, to safeguard its heritage and to guarantee its future.

1. The Shrine of the Book, Jerusalem. For no other nation is a book the centre and focus of its identity as the Bible is for the Jews of Israel. Appropriately, therefore, the Shrine of the Book, built to house the newly discovered biblical manuscripts from the Dead Sea, is a key symbol of the new state and its ethos.

1 INNOCENCE: heroic beginnings

THEODOR HERZL, the founder of modern Zionism, wrote a novel in 1902 elaborating his vision of a Jewish state. The title of the book was *Altneuland* (Old-New Land) and it ended with the phrase 'if you will it, it is no fable'. Forty-six years later, on 14 May, 1948, the state of Israel was reborn. No Jewish state had existed since the year 70 but, for almost nineteen centuries, the dispersed Jews had kept alive the hope of a return to Zion.

Among the complex of elements that combined to bring about the fulfillment of the Zionist dream, none was more potent than Nazi Germany's onslaught against the Jews. The needs of the pitifully few and emaciated survivors of the Holocaust created irresistible pressure for a Jewish homeland. And when Israel declared her independence, the state's first aim was defined as 'the ingathering of the exiles'. The new state was to be a refuge for all Jews and, between 1948 and 1951 more than 300,000 of them arrived from Europe and a slightly greater number from the Muslim lands of Asia and Africa. In three years the Jewish population of Israel more than doubled.

Jews had lived in Muslim countries for centuries but their situation became parlous when Israel's Arab neighbours declared war on the Jewish state. On the very day of Israel's establishment, seven Arab armies launched their attacks and among the victims were their own Jewish communities. Some hastened to Israel through religious fervour, seeing in the new state a realization of the messianic hope. Others came because the implacable hostility of their governments to a Jewish state in the Holy Land raised doubts over their own future.

A herculean task lay before the fledgling state. Simultaneously with its fight for survival, Israel had to absorb the masses of new arrivals. The sick and the aged among them had to be cared for, Jews of all ages, from over fifty nations and with widely differing backgrounds, were to be taught a new language, be housed, found employment, their children educated. A mixed multitude had to be welded into a nation.

Leading his people during this formative period was David Ben-Gurion, a Zionist social-ist, who became Israel's first prime minister. The new state fervently declared its dedication to a parliamentary democracy and put it to the test for the first time at a general election immediately after the conclusion of the War of Independence. That war did not bring peace and ended only with fragile armistice agreements.

Israel's ordeal by combat helped to create a united nation. The young and strong among its citizens, including newcomers, bore the brunt of defence against the attackers. The Haganah, the force organized by the Jews of Palestine before statehood, became the nucleus of the army of Israel. That role was not unchallenged and the first major obstacle was surmounted when Ben-Gurion took decisive and successful action to disarm the underground Jewish fighting groups which had waged their own war both against the British and the Arabs. Defence was, and remained, the key condition for Israel's survival. But survival was only the means for the achievement of the Zionist dream of a just and moral society in their new-old homeland. The Zionist ideal was exemplified in the *kibbutz,* a unique experiment in pioneering and communal living which, after eighty years, still maintained its inspirational role in Israeli society.

The character of the new state was shaped by the Jews from Russia and Poland who, during the first decades of the 20th century, had implemented their Zionist convictions by settling in the harsh environment of long neglected Palestine. They were among the first of the pioneers, working on the land and labouring in trade and industry. The next major category of immigrants were those of their co-religionists who were able to leave Germany before the activation of the Hitler death machine. Then came the mass immigration of the survivors of the death camps and the oriental Jews, all with their own traditions, customs and skills. But all the new Israelis possessed in common an inherited love of learning from which burgeoned Israel's intense and comprehensive cultural life. Not always so constructive were the diverse religious trends which had grown up in almost two thousand years of dispersion as well as the differences in life-style and attitude between religious and secular Jews. Religious controversy became a staple feature in the land of Israel.

In the midst of this ferment of war, absorption and the battle of ideas, and only eight years after its turbulent birth, Israel was faced with the second of its wars, the Suez Campaign of 1956. In collaboration with France and Britain, the Israel Defence Forces occupied the Sinai Peninsula but were compelled to withdraw at the insistence of the government of the United States. It was, however, a condition of withdrawal that the United Nations would maintain a peace-keeping force in the Sinai and that Egypt would not obstruct the use of Eilat, Israel's new port in the Gulf of Aqaba. The abrogation of these provisions by Egypt's President Nasser directly precipitated the Six Day War of 1967.

2, 3, 4. THE HOLOCAUST was, and is still, the crucial event of modern Jewish history, a national trauma that can never be forgotten or ignored. For those Jews whose beliefs were forged amid the horrors of Nazi genocide, the idea of Israel acquired an almost mystical fervour, far transcending normal political passions. *Top:* the ashes of concentration camp victims are laid to rest in Jerusalem, 1948. *Bottom:* paying tribute at the memorial in Israel to the Holocaust, 1973. *Right:* memorial service held in 1961 during the Eichmann trial.

5, 6, 7. THE FIRST IMMIGRANTS after 1948 were displaced persons either from the camps of Central Europe or from Muslim countries hostile to Israel. The new state was committed to the moral duty of accepting any Jew who wanted to come. The result was mass immigration surpassing anything before the war and straining the economy almost to breaking point. These immigrants are arriving at Haifa in 1948 and 1950.

8, 9. THE STATE OF ISRAEL was proclaimed on May 14th 1948, immediately upon the ending of the British mandate and the withdrawal of British troops. The historic meeting, chaired by David Ben-Gurion, took place in Tel-Aviv, beneath a portrait of Theodor Herzl, founder of modern Zionism. Until elections could be held, a provisional government led by Ben-Gurion exercised power. The veteran Chaim Weizmann (seen here voting in 1949) was given the title of President.

10. THE DESTRUCTION of the *Altalena* in June 1948 marked a decisive step in the formation of the new state. The ship was bringing much needed weapons to the Irgun, a Jewish underground army led by Menachem Begin. Ben-Gurion, however, had forbidden anyone to carry arms outside the official army, the Haganah, and when the *Altalena* arrived, it was stormed and destroyed by government troops. For Ben-Gurion, the imposition of central authority was more important than the loss of the arms. Thousands of sightseers came to look at the wreck on the beach of Tel-Aviv.

11, 12, 13. ALL ISRAEL'S NEIGHBOURS immediately declared war: Egypt, Jordan, Syria and Lebanon. Victory was the condition of survival. Both sides had seen war coming; the Arabs had planned and mobilized, the Israelis had bought arms from abroad and trained the Haganah in secret. By May 1948 they could deploy 30,000 troops. These pictures show scenes on the road to Jerusalem.

14. JERUSALEM was the focus of Jewish aspirations. At the beginning of the war it was cut off from the rest of the country and under siege. Ben-Gurion gave its capture top priority, but when a truce was imposed by the United Nations in June 1948, the Jordanians still held the Old City, including the Orthodox Jewish quarter. The division existing at this time became permanent with the signing of the armistices early in 1949.

15, 16. THE FIRST GENERAL ELECTION to be held in Israel took place in January, 1949. The following month the elected Constituent Assembly passed the Transition Law which provided that Israel's legislature was to be a one chamber parliament to be known as the Knesset. The mainly Western electorate of about half a million was politically sophisticated, every shade of opinion being represented by the press.

17, 18. THE FIRST KNESSET met in an old bank building in Jerusalem, adapted to form a debating chamber with a public gallery. There were over ten parties, none with an overall majority, but as the leader of a coalition, Ben-Gurion was secure as prime minister. This photograph was taken in 1956.

תאודור ה.רצל
THEODOR HERZL

19, 20. THE LAW OF RETURN, passed by the Knesset in July 1950, gave every Jew in the world the right to claim Israeli citizenship. The tide of immigration increased. Whole families with children now came, hopeful of a new life and looking forward to the generation to come.

21, 22. RETURN TO THE LAND was the traditional ideal of Zionism from the very beginning. Even before World War I the Jewish National Fund had begun buying land in Galilee. The old stereotype of the Jew – middle-class, intellectual, professional – was to give way to that of the pioneer and the artisan. The dignity of physical work was one of the slogans of the dominant Labour Party.

23, 24. FARMING AND FISHING: two age-old occupations which took on a new dimension of meaning in Israel. The *kibbutz* system harnessed the energy and idealism of young people, but was based upon solid, practical considerations. In the first twenty years of Israel's existence 92% of the land came into public ownership.

25, 26. WATER is the key to agriculture, and the provision of water was too important to be left to private initiative. Between 1948 and 1965 irrigation schemes multiplied the land available to farming by five, from 75,000 to 375,000 acres. Keeping the naturally arid land productive still needs intense effort.

27, 28. MINERALS were almost as important as crops, and the area round the Dead Sea proved to be one of the richest, producing a range of chlorides and other chemicals. The man with the drill is at an opencast copper mine; the factory is near the Dead Sea.

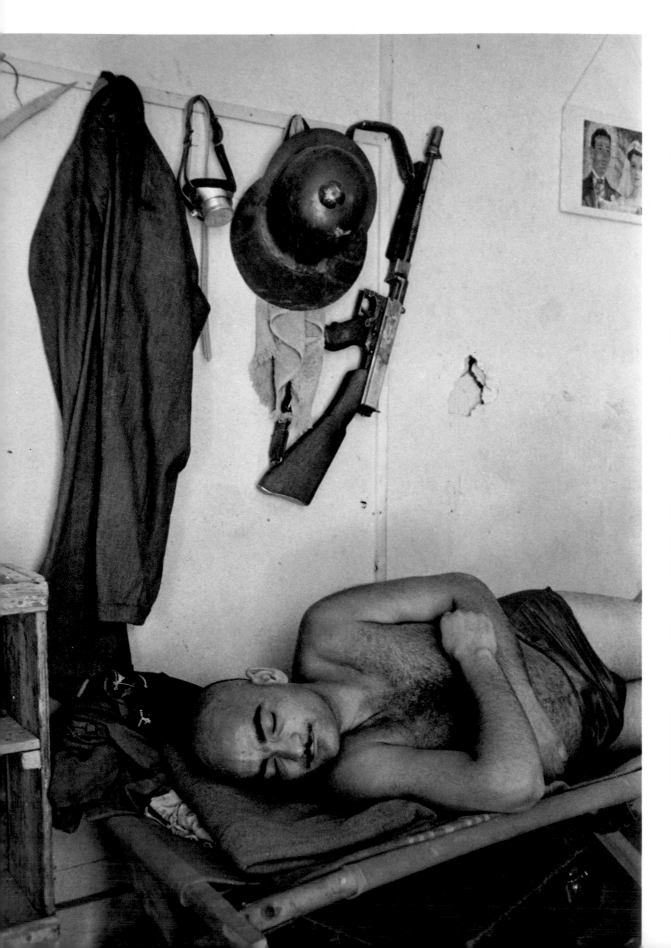

29, 30. KING SOLOMON'S MINES at Timna still yield copper, though in small quantities and of inferior quality. They have been ex- ploited for patriotic rather than economic reasons, and yield about 10,000 tons annually, all exported.

31, 32. POTASH from the Dead Sea was the country's main industry before independence and has been greatly developed since.

33, 34. LEARNING has always been of prime importance in Jewish culture, and education was one of the first preoccupations of the new government. From the beginning, however, it was fraught with ideological conflict. The issue of religious education in immigrant camps split the Knesset in 1951. The children in these pictures, of 1950 and 1951, are learning the Hebrew language.

35, 36. SECULAR TEACHING versus religious – a source of continuing discord. The religious parties, strongly represented in the Knesset, distrusted state education and feared that the younger generation would be wooed away from Orthodoxy, but parents were given the right of choosing between schools conforming to four recognized 'trends'.

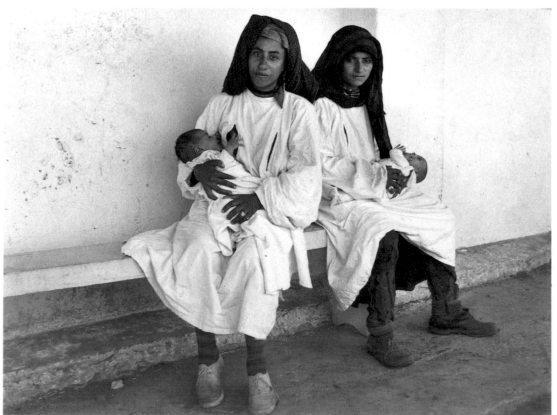

37, 38, 39. 'INTERIOR IMMIGRATION' is the term coined for new births, and as the years pass a greater and greater proportion of Israelis are native born (Sabras). *Left:* new arrivals from the West (Haifa, 1954) and from Arabia (1950). The pram-scape is at Tel-Aviv, 1948.

40, 41. TECHNOLOGY began to transform old Palestine into modern Israel as soon as conditions were settled enough to permit development. High-rise buildings proliferated – first in Tel-Aviv (where in 1965 the Shalom Tower was said to be the tallest building between Milan and Tokyo) and then, to the consternation of many, in ancient cities like Jerusalem. These pictures of the Tel-Aviv beach and of Jerusalem are of 1954.

42, 43. THE SUEZ CAMPAIGN was launched by Israel in October 1956, instigated by Britain and France who planned to intervene in the conflict in order to win back the Suez Canal, recently nationalized by Nasser. That part of the plan was a failure, but Israel succeeded in its object of demoralizing the Egyptians and temporarily occupying the Sinai Peninsula. *Below:* Ben-Gurion and General Dayan.

44, 45. ONE RESULT of the Suez War was an increased influx of Jewish immigrants from Egypt, where Jews had lived from time immemorial. Now they had to flee, coming to Israel via Greece by sea or by air. *Above:* Egyptian Jews worshipping in Israel; *right,* Haifa Airport.

46, 47. CHILDREN OF Egyptian Jews, welcomed in Israel in 1957 and preparing to become staunch Israeli citizens.

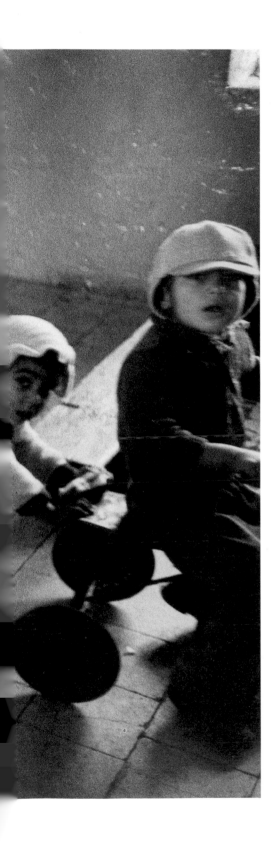

48, 49. BEN-GURION, the father of the Israeli state, resigned in 1963 over the so-called Lavon Affair (Lavon was a minister forced out of office in 1955 for his alleged responsibility for a 'security mishap'). Ben-Gurion retired to his *kibbutz* in the Negev – a symbolic act intended to inspire others to follow. With his dominating presence removed, a new generation of his associates in the Labour Party came to power, including Golda Meir, later to become prime minister.

50, 51. THE QUALITY OF LIFE in Israel was in a state of permanent revolution. New immigrants brought their own skills and traditions, but in spite of wide differences, the prevailing ethos was that of the technically advanced West. *Left:* an Orthodox wedding. *Above:* street scene in Tel-Aviv.

52, 53. THE ARTS flourished in the early days of Israel, though public taste was not always as enlightened as its sponsors might wish. Museums and picture galleries received generous government support. In 1966 an important Picasso exhibition was held at Tel-Aviv. Its opening (*right*) was a grand occasion. Some of the later visitors (*above*) were not quite so sure.

54, 55. As the most advanced country in the Middle East, Israel was keenly aware of technological advances and proud of its own contributions. *Below:* a welfare clinic in Tel-Aviv. *Right:* an exhibition to show government social services in housing, care for the aged and industrial safety.

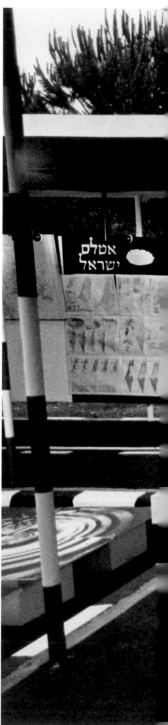

56, 57. THE PAST is more alive in Israel than in any other country, virtually every region having incalculable significance not only to the Jews themselves but to the adherents of the other two 'religions of the Book', Christianity and Islam. Near the Sea of Galilee stands the ruins of a second-century synagogue of Capernaum (*below*), a site where Jesus preached. *Right:* by the same shore, a group of Druses, an Arab sect which broke away from Islam in the eleventh century and claimed to be descendants of Jethro. They have been admitted to full Israeli citizenship, but are not Jews.

58, 59. OLD BELIEFS live on, untouched by the modern world. Jews had always come to Palestine to die – now they came to live and to study. *Below:* students at a Talmudic school in Jerusalem. *Right:* an Arab woman in the Old City makes the same gesture to hide her face from the camera.

60, 61. JEWISH FESTIVALS became to some
extent secularized, like Christmas in the
Christian world. Purim, a time of merry-
making, is celebrated by these Jewish
children in angel costumes as a com-
memoration of Queen Esther's salvation of
her people, but to the Arabs (*left*) it is simp-
ly an excuse to dress up.

62, 63. JERUSALEM, sacred to three religions, tenuously preserves its past amid the threats of modernization and of war. *Right:* Christian pilgrims follow the Via Dolorosa, Christ's route from judgement to crucifixion.

64, 65, 66. THE FIRST KIBBUTZ was founded in 1909 and its way of life became an
image of utopian socialism, with all goods
held in common and every man and woman
contributing to the common welfare. After
the foundation of Israel, *kibbutzim* served as
fortresses in exposed areas threatened by
enemy attack. (*Above:* an armoured car pat-
rols the fields near the Jordanian border in
1967.) They were also mirrors of the cosmo-
politan society, young people from the
West happily rubbing shoulders with immigrants from the Yemen (*right*).

67, 68. AFTER TWENTY YEARS Israel was flourishing in every sense: most obviously in the purely physical change that had come over the landscape, where trees and vegetable crops covered land that had previously been desert. *Below:* by the Lake of Tiberias. *Right:* olive groves in Samaria.

2 EXPERIENCE: the realities of power

THE SIX DAY WAR was a pre-emptive strike by Israel after President Nasser of Egypt had demanded, and achieved, the withdrawal of the United Nations Emergency Force from the Sinai border with Israel and imposed a blockade of Israel's southern port of Eilat. Israel was faced with its gravest threat since the War of Independence as Egypt and Syria massed their forces for attack. Tension grew in the ensuing weeks while Israel and her friends desperately sought a diplomatic solution to the crisis, seen at the time as the menace of a second Holocaust. When Israel's leaders concluded that such help would not be forthcoming, they launched a series of surprise attacks on 5 June 1967 which, in the space of three hours, destroyed the air forces of Egypt, Jordan and Syria.

With the complete air superiority secured by its first days' success, the Israeli land forces moved against the armies of her three Arab antagonists and, by June 11, had routed them. By the time of the cease-fire, Israel was in occupation of territory from all three of her enemies. Jordan had lost the area of the West Bank of the river Jordan, Syria the Golan Heights and Egypt the Sinai peninsula and the Gaza Strip.

The Six Day War constituted one of the most brilliant military operations in history. But for all Jews, not alone the Israelis, its greatest triumph was the reunification of Jerusalem, the focus of millennia of Jewish hopes and prayers. The city had been divided by the War of Independence armistice line which left a great part in Jordanian hands including Judaism's most hallowed site, the Western Wall of the Second Temple. While all or some of the occupied territories could be returned as part of a peace settlement, Israel insisted that it would not relinquish united Jerusalem as its capital though it guaranteed access for all faiths whose holy places would be safeguarded.

It was Israel's intention to make its military occupation of the captured territories the most humane in history. General Dayan, the Minister of Defence who bore responsibility for their administration, ordered the Israeli forces to be unobtrusive, directed that Jordanian law would continue on the West Bank and that the bridges linking West Bank to Jordan should be kept open. In spite of General Dayan's policies, Israel found the role of an occupying power to be inherently unsympathetic. Occupation inevitably provoked resistance which in turn prompted repression. The international acclaim for Israel's victory in war did not survive for long after the occupation.

Within the Jewish state the Six Day War stimulated profound changes. Israelis felt safer with the protective depth of the occupied territories as buffer zones. Some Israelis decided to settle in the West Bank which religious and political zealots regarded as part of greater Israel. With the occupation came a new and intense polarization between the so-called doves who were ready to trade territory for peace and the hawks asserting the rights of conquest or of historical title.

Israel now faced a world increasingly critical of its occupation policies and with it the no less testing intensification of Palestinian nationalism. Growing Arab hostility and the perception that they stood alone led many Israelis into the adoption of extremist attitudes. More positively, the transformed situation after the war also produced among Israelis a deepening of Jewish consciousness and an appreciation of the long and often tragic history of their people.

After the Six Day War Israelis experienced a steadily improving standard of living as new industries developed and tourism flourished. In the postwar euphoria, the politicians, the public and, not least, the defence forces became dangerously complacent. That was shattered on 6 October, 1973, Yom Kippur, the holiest day in the Jewish calendar, when the Egyptian and Syrian air and land forces launched their own surprise attack on Israel, an assault for which the Israelis were unprepared. Military intelligence had rejected the probability of war in spite of the reports of movement of enemy troops. Only a small proportion of Israel's army consists of professionals. The bulk is comprised of citizens who can be rapidly mobilized but on this occasion, in the national mood of relaxation, the delay in mobilization led to near disaster.

The war lasted almost three weeks and for the first few days Israel's situation appeared desperate. But before the end of the first week, successful counterattacks took Israeli forces across the Suez Canal into Egypt and into Syrian territory. When the cease-fire came, Israel had averted a calamity but had suffered heavy casualties. However, Egypt's initial successes in the war and the honourable armistice mainly achieved by the negotiating skills of Mr Henry Kissinger, America's Secretary of State, restored national self-confidence and led directly to the historic breakthrough brought about by President Sadat's initiative in November 1977.

69, 70. THE SIX DAY WAR (June 5th-10th, 1967) was an offensive undertaken in self-defence. In May 1967 it had become clear that President Nasser of Egypt intended to deliver a decisive blow against Israel; after requesting that all United Nations forces should withdraw from its border with Israel he replaced them with his own troops poised to invade Israel from the south, while Syria and Jordan attacked from the north. Israel determined to act first, and did so with a success that astonished even

themselves. In six days, they had pushed
back their frontiers against each of their
enemies – taking the whole of Sinai and the
Gaza strip from Egypt, the area between
Jerusalem and the Jordan (the so-called
West Bank) from Jordan and the Golan
Heights from Syria.

71, 72. THE WESTERN WALL, for Jews the most sacred spot in the world, was the most emotive of all the gains of the Six Day War. By annexing the territory west of the river Jordan, Israel abolished the hated division of Jerusalem and regained the Old City, prohibited to Jews for nearly twenty years. The upper picture shows the long pilgrimage to the Wall on the first day that it was accessible.

73. WITHIN HOURS of Israeli forces reuniting Jerusalem, the Wall was opened up to the thousands of pilgrims who flocked from all over the country. Arab houses that had clustered round it were bull-dozed and a new open space created. The Wall itself is what remains of the substructure of Herod's Temple built in the first century BC. The emotional euphoria generated at this time temporarily obscured the problems which annexation of the new territories would bring for the future.

אסור להדליק נרות
במקום קדוש זה
בפקודה:
הרבנות הצבאית הראשית

74, 75. HOLY PLACES: a wounded soldier is helped to the Wall by two of his comrades and (*below*) Israeli soldiers guarding the entrance to the Church of the Holy Sepulchre, watched by Greek Orthodox monks. Freedom of religion was now proclaimed for all three faiths – Judaism, Christianity and Islam. Jordan's guardianship of the Holy Places had not been exemplary.

76, 77. JEWS FLOCKED to the Wall in a wave of emotion in which patriotism and religious devotion were intermingled. *Left:* a night vigil by Orthodox Jews. Muslims too could participate in the new freedom, and Israeli Arabs (*right*) who had been cut off from the Dome of the Rock during the years of division were able to visit their own Holy Places.

78. THERE WAS GRIEF and anxiety in the midst of victory. The mood was serious, a mood reflected in the faces of this crowd at the funeral of soldiers killed in the war, where rifles and military uniforms mingle with tributes to the dead and symbols of faith.

79, 80. MILITARY SUCCESS had been the result of careful planning. The Sinai campaign had been worked out by Yitzhak Rabin, the chief of staff (*left*), but he relinquished command to Moshe Dayan, who was given most of the credit. Dayan is seen (*above*) talking to Teddy Kollek, then (and still) mayor of Jerusalem.

81, 82. THE MANDELBAUM GATE, named after an obscure individual the site of whose house it occupied, was a breach in the frontier between the two halves of Jerusalem. From 1948 to 1967 it was the only communication. By 1967, when these photographs were taken, it had ceased to be of political significance.

83, 84. THE ISRAELI-JORDAN border was now the river Jordan, but Israel – and especially the minister responsible for the West Bank, Moshe Dayan – had no wish to seal Israel off from its neighbour. The only link was the Allenby Bridge, which Dayan kept open to allow Arabs on both banks to keep in contact. Thousands used it, in spite of Israel's necessary security precautions.

85, 86, 87. On the West Bank, Arab life went on as before, and many of those who had fled returned (*right*). Its Muslim inhabitants were to benefit from the standard of life enjoyed by Israel, but the problem of their political rights still had not been solved.

88, 89, 90. THE GAZA STRIP posed a different problem. The inhabitants were Palestinians, not Egyptians, but their way of life was still Middle Eastern.

91, 92. SINAI was the largest of the territories annexed by Israel after the Six Day War.
It was mostly arid desert inhabited by Bedouin. For the Jews, however, it was a place
of great historical interest, and much
archaeological work was done here before
Israel restored it to Egypt in 1978.

93, 94. JEWS AND ARABS had to achieve a closer working relationship than before. *Left:* Orthodox Jews negotiate with an Arab taxi-driver. *Above:* Hasidim could emerge from their enclosed environment where they had remained on sufferance during the Jordanian occupation.

95, 96. As the years passed the *kibbut-zim* could not help changing in character. Those shown here are run by Yemenite Jews (*left*) and Moroccans (*below*).

97, 98. THE NEW KIBBUTZIM kept pace with the standards of living in the towns. These were even industrial ones which – contrary to their early principles – employed hired labour. But many features of those first years were preserved, such as communal child-rearing.

99, 100. THE PAST is never far away in Israel. Here a party of workers in the fields take part in the ancient spring festival. *Above:* young Orthodox Jews at the barbers.

101, 102. MUSIC – perhaps the most essentially Jewish of the arts – has been given lavish official encouragement. *Right:* the Abu Ghosh music festival. *Opposite:* Haifa Symphony Orchestra.

103. THE ROCK OF MASADA is the symbol of Israel. It was here that the last Jewish nation was extinguished in AD 73, a nation of which the statesmen of 1948 saw themselves as the lineal inheritors. Here too the Jews attained their highest peak of heroism, when – overwhelmed by vastly superior Roman forces and after a siege lasting many months – the defenders committed communal suicide rather than submit. In no other place is the defiant spirit of modern Israel so vividly present.

104, 105. THE DEAD SEA SCROLLS, though first discovered in 1947, only gradually emerged as one of the great historical discoveries of modern times. As more and more of the caves above Qumran were explored (this rope-climber is operating in 1964), manuscripts of biblical texts, notably Isaiah, came to light that were centuries older than any previously known. In the heady atmosphere after the Six Day War, it seemed yet another confirmation of Israel's destiny.

מערת מגיל
(מס' NO. 4)

ROLLS CAVE

مغارة الاسفار

106, 107. ARCHAEOLOGY is a national passion. To the average Israeli, the investigation of the past is not just an academic pursuit; it has resonances for the present, and even overt political ramifications. Should not what was Jewish two thousand years ago be Jewish today? *Left:* excavating a fort on the Israeli-Sinai border. *Above:* Yigal Yadin, archaeologist and soldier, digging at Hazor.

108, 109. NOT BY CHANCE was one of the
most exposed of the *kibbutzim* named Masada. *Above:* members of the settlement killed
by a terrorist mine are buried. *Left:* at a
nearby *kibbutz* a family shelters from Syrian
shells. Israel is still a nation under siege,
with the farms often in the front line.

110, 111, 112. IN THE OLD CITIES of Israel the traditions are still those of the Middle Eastern world common to Islamic countries, even if many of the inhabitants and shopkeepers are Jewish.

113, 114. THE CONTRAST between East and West, ancient and modern, is one of the paradoxical attractions that bring travellers to Israel. Such juxtapositions occur everywhere all the time. Here – wedding dresses among the Yemenite Jews and in the smart shops of Tel-Aviv.

115, 116. THE AIRCRAFT INDUSTRY owes part of its impetus to the fear that Western countries might suddenly cut off vital supplies of arms, as France did after the Six Day War. Beginning from nothing in 1953, with seventy workers, it began to produce wholly Israeli aircraft in 1965 and by 1971 employed 13,500 people.

117, 118, 119. THE YOM KIPPUR WAR, the fourth war that Israel had fought in twenty-five years, took the country completely by surprise. Still humiliated by their defeat in 1967, Egypt and Syria struck without warning in October 1973, during the festival of Yom Kippur, the Day of Atonement, the holiest day in the Jewish calendar. It was almost disaster. The Israeli army sustained heavy losses and was forced to retreat. Only desperate counter-attacks on all fronts turned the tide.

120, 121. THE ISRAELIS were used to capturing large numbers of prisoners, less used to becoming prisoners themselves (*above*). During the Yom Kippur War they had to face the humiliating spectacle of Israeli soldiers being paraded in Cairo for the benefit of Egyptian television. *Right:* Egyptian soldiers captured near the Suez Canal.

122, 123. WAR had broken out on October 6th, 1973. By the 14th, the Syrians were in full retreat and the way to Damascus lay open, and by the 21st the Egyptians had been pushed to the other side of the Suez Canal. Here a service is held next to the Canal and (right) Israeli troops gaze across into Egypt. Once again Israeli military expertise had triumphed.

3 HOPE: problems and achievements

ALTHOUGH THE YOM KIPPUR WAR ended in victory for Israel, it had been a close run thing. Israeli losses had been heavy and, in response to mounting public disquiet, a commission of inquiry was set up. Its report, pointing to errors in judgment and slackness in organization stimulated the peaceful revolution of May 1977, when a general election ended Labour's rule, replacing it with that of the right-wing Likud grouping led by Mr Menahem Begin.

Unpreparedness for the Yom Kippur War was only one of the causes of the surprising election result. The electorate clearly believed that the time had come for a change. Even as living standards rose so did apprehension at the effect of escalating inflation. Moreover, the Labour party had been so long in power that it had become susceptible to many of the failings which accompany entrenched authority. Israel's democratic system demonstrated that it could work effectively to bring about change.

The character of the country was itself changing as the Jews of Middle Eastern and North African origin (the oriental Jews) became a majority of Israel's Jewish population. With the passage of time they began to play a greater part in political life and challenged the European monopoly of leadership. The oriental Jews had made a substantial contribution to Mr Begin's electoral success in 1977 by which time Labour had come to be seen as the party of the establishment, dedicated to the maintenance of an unsatisfactory status quo.

The power of the religious minority increased. The oriental Jews tended to be more religiously observant than the Europeans while many immigrants from the USSR, long cut off from their fellow Jews and inspired by the creation and achievements of the Jewish state, had returned to the practice of Judaism. A religious and Zionist resurgence had taken place in the Soviet Union and many thousands of Russian Jews sought to join their people in the Land of Israel.

By the time Mr Begin assumed office, the substantial immigration from the USSR had ended. Linked with the official Russian attitude to Jewish emigration was their support for the Arab cause. An amelioration of the Arab-Israel conflict could have re-opened the doors. That suddenly became a serious possibility when President Sadat publicly declared his desire for peace with Israel and offered to travel to Jerusalem. The Begin government had been perceived as unwilling to compromise on the return of the occupied territories. But when President Sadat had made it clear that no solution would be possible without territorial compromise, Mr Begin was in a better position to respond favourably than a Labour government. Had Labour been in power, its flexibility on this issue would have been limited by domestic considerations. Mr Begin's party would have been, perhaps literally, up in arms had Labour offered to return territory.

As it was, it was Mr Begin who, with overwhelming support from all parties, welcomed the Egyptian leader on his arrival in Jerusalem, introduced him to the Knesset and later agreed, in the Camp David Accords, to return the territory captured in 1967 from the Egyptians in exchange for peace. That treaty with the most populous and distinguished of the Arab nations introduced a dramatic change in the long static Israel-Arab conflict. All Israelis hoped that it would break the log-jam which had for so long obstructed a rational solution.

That was not to be swiftly accomplished but the Camp David Accords initiated a peace process which, slowly and haltingly, stumbled forward. In an endeavour to destroy the power of the Palestine Liberation Organisation, Israel, which saw it as a major obstacle to peace, in 1982 invaded the Lebanon where the PLO was based. The national debate provoked by this controversial war led to the resignation of Mr Begin, to the loss of power by his party and to the formation in 1984 of the Government of National Unity.

Throughout its existence, Israel had lived under the unrelenting tensions of a nation at war. Nevertheless, except in issues where national security was involved, the democratic rights and freedoms of its citizens were cherished. Nor had war diminished the remarkable vitality of the Jewish state in every aspect of work and leisure.

Excluding the occupied territories, the population of Israel in 1987 consisted of 3.5 million Jews and 600,000 Arabs. Among them were believers in every variation of the Jewish, Christian and Muslim faiths as well as many others. Conflicts erupted from time to time, but religious freedom remained unimpaired.

Democracy flourished and the rule of law prevailed. Israel's legal system, independent of the executive, became the ultimate champion of individual rights. A vigorous and extensive press as well as radio and television were also independent of government control. Israeli writers, artists and scholars lived and worked in a climate which appreciated and encouraged their endeavours. The welfare programmes introduced by the socialist founders of the Jewish state ensured that essential needs of the population were met. The educational system, though beset by problems of content and funding, remained comprehensive and free. And, for a country of its size, its seven thriving universities were a symbol of its dedication to learning and progress.

The age-old Jewish dream of a return to Zion had been realized. But on its fortieth anniversary there remain many unfulfilled goals, among them peace and security and the reconciliation of political, religious and social differences. Herzl's successors have still to overcome daunting challenges if they are to see the full flowering of his vision.

124, 125. THE YOM KIPPUR WAR had left all three combatant countries exhausted. People were ready for compromise in the cause of peace, and after three years of tentative negotiations, President Sadat of Egypt made the decisive move. In October 1977, in a dramatic and unprecedented gesture, he flew to Jerusalem and addressed the Knesset on the theme of reconciliation. *Below:* Sadat being welcomed at Ben-Gurion Airport by Mrs Golda Meir, then in opposition (Begin was prime minister). Sadat's initiative led to the Camp David Accords. The mood in Tel-Aviv (*right*) was overwhelmingly for peace. In September 1979 a treaty was signed with Egypt.

126, 127, 128. CHURCH AND STATE — age-old faith and modern democracy — are the two cornerstones of modern Israel. Symbolic of Judaism are the great *Menorah* (seven-branched candlestick) that stands opposite the Knesset in Jerusalem and the Shrine of the Book (*below*), where the most ancient manuscripts of the Bible can be read. *Right:* the Israel Museum with the new Knesset building in the background.

129, 130, 131. IN THE MIDST of religious differences, there is complete freedom of religious practice. *Above:* a Samaritan, a sect that is Jewish in origin, but neither Jewish nor Christian in doctrine. *Below:* Ethiopian Jews on a pilgrimage. *Right:* the Tomb of Abraham at Hebron, sacred to Christians, Muslims and Jews.

132, 133. SAFED, in the north of Israel, was once, in the sixteenth century, the home of Jewish cabbalistic mysticism, and still has an old quarter (*below*) where the modern world has had little impact. It has been developed as a new town and, because of its strategic position, as a potential defence against invasion. It also includes an artists' colony and a textile factory.

שער
10
GATE
החברה
AIRLINE
טיסה
FLIGHT
מתוכנן
SCHEDULED
מתוקן
REVISED

134, 135. MANY of today's immigrants come from Russia and their numbers seem likely to increase. *Left:* arriving at the airport. *Right:* receiving instruction in a machine shop.

136, 137. THE CHILDREN, citizens of tomorrow's Israel, inherit a more uniform cultural background than did their parents. Schools differ according to religious group-ings, but educational standards apply nationwide. *Left:* on the *kibbutz* of Givat-Haim. *Above:* young immigrants from Georgia.

138, 139. THE GENERATIONS find themselves separated by memories, by experience and by expectation. *Left:* one of the pioneer farmers. *Below:* members of the Degania *kibbutz,* the first to be founded in what was then Palestine.

140, 141, 142. THREE STEPS towards a
higher standard of living: the 1940s (a camp
at Haifa), the 1950s, and 1980s (Falashas
from Ethiopia).

143, 144. ARABS LIVING UNDER ISRAELI rule are still only partially assimilated, and their future is closely tied to the solution of the Palestinian problem. The Bedouin of Sinai (*left*), however, have largely accepted the new situation (here a Bedouin boy writes down their new address for his father). Many Yemenite Jews (*below*) easily adapted themselves to life in Tel-Aviv.

145, 146, 147. EDUCATION has kept pace with progress. In the early days (*opposite*) children were taught on a blackboard in the open air. Now texts can be studied on a computer – the screen *below* displays the opening words of *Genesis*. For religious purposes, however, the Bible still has to be handwritten on a scroll (*left*).

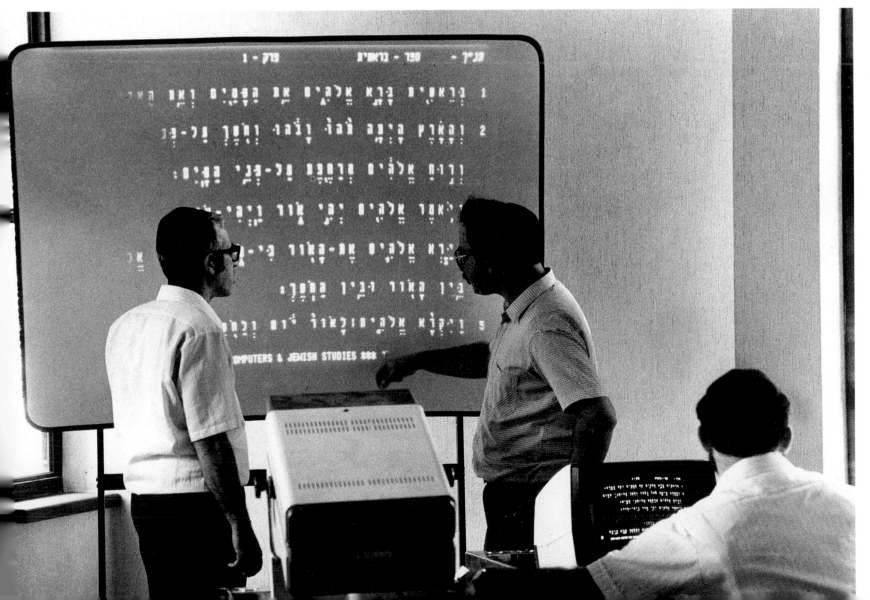

148, 149. IN THE OLD QUARTERS, life remains constant for a generation which has
itself grown old. *Above:* Orthodox Jews
near Tel-Aviv. *Right:* Christians in the Old
City of Jerusalem.

150, 151. TOMORROW'S CITIZENS in the city of yesterday. Two byways in Jerusalem . . .Jews, Arabs or Christians?

152, 153. WHILE DELVING INTO THE PAST and preserving its heritage, Israel has transformed the land with new buildings, primarily to house its increasing population, but also with an eye to territorial settlement and defence. *Below*: archaeologists working on the city wall, Jerusalem. *Right*: a new satellite outside Jerusalem's wall.

154, 155. PARTS OF THE OLD CITY of
Jerusalem (*left*) and other ancient cities
such as Jaffa have been meticulously restored with expert archaeological advice.
Nearby rise notable works of modern
architecture such as the Kennedy Memorial
(*above*).

156, 157. THE WORLD COMES TO ISRAEL either as pilgrims or tourists. Tourism is now a major industry, benefitting not only the state as a whole but also the mainly Arab shopkeepers of the picturesque markets. The photographs are both of Jerusalem.

158, 159, 160. RELIGION AS BUSINESS.
These pictures tell their own story. The
man above supplies holy objects, in particular the box-like phylacteries worn by
Orthodox Jews on their foreheads for
prayer.

161, 162. TWO UNEXPECTED NEWCOMERS to the Israeli economy: crocodiles and ostriches, both farmed for profit on specialized *kibbutzim*.

163, 164, 165. THE PALM has played a part in symbolic ritual since the dawn of Judaism, and is still rich in associations for both Jew and Christian. *Below:* growing palm trees on a *kibbutz* south of the Dead Sea. On the Feast of Tabernacles, the palm, willow and myrtle are tied together. *Top right:* the willow remaining from this wreath. *Bottom right:* Palm Sunday procession, the Christian festival corresponding to Passover.

166, 167, 168. WAVES OF IMMIGRANTS
continue to add to the cultural mix of Israel,
making it – paradoxically – the most multi-
racial society in the world.

169, 170. THE HEBREW UNIVERSITY was the first to be established in Jewish Palestine. Founded in 1925, it had 900 students at the time of independence. In 1949 it was forced to move from its site on Mount Scopus, but continued to grow, and in 1970 reoccupied its old campus. By 1986 it had over 16,000 students.

171, 172. ISRAEL'S NEWEST UNIVERSITY
is the University of the Negev, rising from
the arid desert at Beersheba. It was founded
in 1965 and contains some of the boldest of
Israel's modern buildings.

173, 174. THE NEW LAW. Founded as it is on a Talmudic base with British and Ottoman ingredients, and confronted by problems of rights, liberties and procedures more serious than in any old-established country, the Israeli legal system is a fascinating subject in itself. *Below:* a petition-writer in Tel-Aviv. *Right:* waiting-room of a modern courthouse, also Tel-Aviv.

175, 176. THE OLD LAW. In the religious communities the ancient Law which has served for centuries continues to be interpreted and applied. *Above:* a rabbi expounding the Talmud for a student. *Right:* an Armenian priest teaching a disciple.

תושלום עכשיו

תושלום עכשיו

לי"ש את המסקנות קדימאון!

יחוד

177, 178. THE SEARCH for peace consistent with security has exercised every Israeli government since 1948. Compromise and conciliation have to be balanced against the need for strength. *Left:* a meeting with Bedouin in the Negev desert to discuss peaceful co-existence. *Above:* to the younger generation, disillusioned with Israel's role in Lebanon, peace initiatives are not being pursued energetically enough. They demand 'Peace Now.'

179. PREPARATION FOR WAR is not incon-
sistent with the desire for peace – most of
Israel's wars have been pre-emptive strikes
to anticipate attack. The invasion of Lebanon aimed to destroy the PLO strongholds
across the northern border. Carried beyond
this limited goal, however, the army became drawn into what has been called
'Israel's Vietnam.'

180, 181. ANOTHER WAR – the longest in Israel's long history – has been man against the desert. Most of the land is naturally infertile. The only victory that counts is that which brings life. These Hasidim (*above*) are visiting the district round Jericho in 1967. *Right:* the road from Jerusalem to Hebron.

182, 183. TO BRING FERTILITY where nothing had grown before is Israel's perennial mission – hence the zeal with which marginal land is brought under cultivation, trees planted and crops harvested.

184. THE NEGEV has become a symbol of the struggle against natural obstacles. Here the Zionist dream, whatever changes and compromises it has undergone elsewhere, remains intact. 'Just as the Negev contains hidden resources, so does man,' said Ben-Gurion when he returned here as a private citizen in 1963; 'but it is in the Negev that man can become conscious of his hidden powers.'

OUTLINE CHRONOLOGY

14 May 1948   Declaration of the establishment of the state of Israel with David Ben-Gurion as Prime Minister. *De facto* recognition by USA. Five Arab states invade Israel.

15 May 1948   Termination of the British mandate over Palestine.

18 May 1948   *De jure* recognition of Israel by the USSR.

25 Jan 1949   First Israeli general election.

29 Jan 1949   *De facto* recognition of Israel by the UK.

17 Feb 1949   Chaim Weizmann becomes first President of Israel.

24 Feb 1949   Israel and Egypt sign armistice agreement in Rhodes ending the War of Independence.

10 March 1949   Ben-Gurion forms first elected coalition government.

11 May 1949   Israel admitted to the UN.

8 Nov 1949   Operation Magic Carpet begins, flying 50,000 Yemenite Jews to Israel.

13 Dec 1949   Jerusalem proclaimed capital of Israel.

5 July 1950   Knesset enacts Law of Return.

15 July 1951   Completion of 'Operation Ezra and Nehemia,' bringing to Israel over 100,000 Jews from Iraq.

10 Sept 1952   Luxembourg reparations agreement signed between West Germany and Israel.

9 Nov 1952   Death of Chaim Weizmann.

13 Feb 1953   Soviets break diplomatic relations with Israel to be resumed after death of Stalin.

29 Oct 1956   Launching of Sinai Campaign.

11 May 1960   Capture of Adolf Eichmann in Argentina.

31 May 1962   Eichmann executed in Jerusalem.

16 June 1963   Ben-Gurion resigns.

5 June 1967   Six Day War begins.

1 Sept 1967   Arab summit in Khartoum adopts 'no recognition, no negotiation, no peace' with Israel resolution.

7 March 1969   Golda Meir becomes Prime Minister.

10 June 1973   German Chancellor Willy Brandt visits Israel, the first by a German Premier.

6 Oct 1973   Yom Kippur War begins.

24 Oct 1973   Yom Kippur War cease-fire.

1 Dec 1973   Death of David Ben-Gurion.

20 May 1977   Menahem Begin takes office as Prime Minister at the head of the first Likud-led government.

19 Nov 1977	Egyptian President Anwar Sadat arrives in Jerusalem.
17 Sep 1978	Begin and Sadat sign Camp David Accords.
29 March 1979	Peace Treaty between Egypt and Israel signed in Washington to come into effect on 25 Nov 1979.
25 Jan 1980	Completion of first stage of Israel's withdrawal from Sinai.
25 Apr 1982	Completion of final stage of Israel's withdrawal from Sinai.
6 June 1982	Israel invades Lebanon in 'Operation Peace for Galilee'.
17 May 1983	Israel and Lebanon sign peace treaty to be abrogated by Lebanon.
13 Sept 1984	Shimon Peres becomes Prime Minister of a Government of National Unity on a rotation basis with Itzhak Shamir, leader of Likud.
3 Jan 1985	Disclosure in Jerusalem of 'Operation Moses', the airlift of 25,000 Jews from Ethiopia.
16 Apr 1985	Israel approves withdrawal of troops from Lebanon to be completed by 6 June.
20 Oct 1986	Rotation completed successfully. Shamir becomes Prime Minister and Peres Foreign Minister.

Titlepage: Leonard Freed, 1967

1. Micha Bar-Am, 1975
2. Robert Capa, 1948
3. Micha Bar-Am, 1973
4. Erich Hartmann, 1961
5. Robert Capa, 1948
6. Robert Capa, 1948
7. Robert Capa, 1950
8. Robert Capa, 1948
9. Robert Capa, 1948
10. Robert Capa, 1948
11. Robert Capa, 1948
12. Robert Capa, 1948
13. Robert Capa, 1948
14. Burt Glinn, 1948
15. Robert Capa, 1949
16. Robert Capa, 1949
17. Robert Capa, 1948
18. Burt Glinn, 1956
19. David Seymour, 1954
20. Robert Capa, 1948
21. Robert Capa, 1948
22. Robert Capa, 1948
23. David Seymour, 1952
24. David Seymour, 1954
25. Burt Glinn, 1956
26. Leonard Freed, 1967
27. David Seymour, 1952
28. Leonard Freed, 1962
29. David Seymour, 1952
30. David Seymour, 1952
31. Leonard Freed, 1967
32. Leonard Freed, 1962
33. Robert Capa, 1950
34. David Seymour, 1951
35. Micha Bar-Am, 1958
36. Burt Glinn, 1957
37. David Seymour, 1954
38. Robert Capa, 1950
39. Robert Capa, 1948
40. David Seymour, 1954
41. David Seymour, 1954
42. Burt Glinn, 1967
43. Micha Bar-Am, 1957
44. Burt Glinn, 1957
45. Burt Glinn, 1957
46. Burt Glinn, 1957
47. Burt Glinn, 1957
48. Micha Bar-Am, 1971
49. Micha Bar-Am, 1970
50. Robert Capa, 1949
51. Erich Hartmann, 1961
52. Micha Bar-Am, 1966
53. Micha Bar-Am, 1966
54. Patrick Zachmann, 1977
55. Leonard Freed, 1967
56. Leonard Freed, 1967
57. Micha Bar-Am, 1968
58. Robert Capa, 1948
59. Leonard Freed, 1967
60. Leonard Freed, 1968
61. Leonard Freed, 1967
62. Inge Morath, 1956
63. George Rodger, 1952
64. Leonard Freed, 1967
65. Leonard Freed, 1967
66. Leonard Freed, 1967
67. René Burri, 1963
68. Erich Lessing, 1973
69. Micha Bar-Am, 1967
70. Micha Bar-Am, 1967
71. Leonard Freed, 1967
72. Marilyn Silverstone, 1967
73. Patrick Zachmann, 1977
74. Leonard Freed, 1967
75. Leonard Freed, 1967
76. Micha Bar-Am, 1967
77. Leonard Freed, 1967
78. Leonard Freed, 1967
79. Leonard Freed, 1967
80. Leonard Freed, 1967
81. Leonard Freed, 1967
82. Leonard Freed, 1967
83. Leonard Freed, 1967
84. Micha Bar-Am, 1968
85. Raymond Depardon, 1974
86. Raymond Depardon, 1975
87. Leonard Freed, 1967
88. Cornell Capa, 1967
89. Micha Bar-Am, 1969
90. Leonard Freed, 1967
91. Micha Bar-Am, 1970
92. René Burri, 1967

INDEX

Numbers in Roman type refer to pages; in italic to illustrations.